Frog Day

After school, Sam looked at a poster on the library wall. It said that help was needed to clean up the pond at Sun Park on Frog Day. The frogs were dying.

Sam's class was doing
a project called "Save It!"

"We could save the frogs
at Sun Park," said Sam
to himself.

So he wrote down
the telephone number
from the poster.

FROG DAY

GW00792749

Sun Park

On October 5th, International Frog Day, people all around the world will be helping to save dying frogs. Hop along to Sun Park on Saturday and help us clean up the pond for Sun Park's frogs.

Tel: 555 9024

5

The next day, Sam told his teacher and class about the poster and the Sun Park frogs.

"October the 5th is this Saturday. Who would like to help clean up the pond and save the frogs on Frog Day?" Mrs. Webb asked the class.

Everyone put up their hands.

At lunchtime, Sam and Mrs. Webb telephoned the people who put up the poster. Mrs. Webb spoke to a man named Mr. Johnson. She told him that her class would love to help.

Then she wrote down the time when Mr. Johnson would meet them at the pond.

After lunch, the children wrote letters to take home. They asked their families if some of them would like to help, too.

On Saturday, Mrs. Webb, the children, and some adult helpers went to Sun Park.

Mr. Johnson met them by the pond and thanked them for coming. He gave out some plastic bags, nets, buckets, and rubber gloves.

Everyone got into groups. There was an adult helper in every group, and each group had a different job.

Sam went with Mrs. Webb. His group had to pick up litter around the pond.

13

Mr. Johnson's group had to pull out the weeds that were growing at the edge of the pond. The weeds were slippery and slimy. Everyone had to be careful not to fall in.

15

When they were finished, Mr. Johnson called everyone together. He showed them how to plant reeds.

"These will help us make a good home for the frogs," said Mr. Johnson. "And now for the best part of the day."

Then Mr. Johnson gave each child a plastic bag full of tadpoles.
Everyone followed
Mr. Johnson to the pond to let the tadpoles go.

After watching the tadpoles enjoy their new home, Sam's class sat down to eat a snack. Everyone was very careful not to drop any litter.

21

When they had finished eating, Mrs. Webb stood up. "Thank you, everyone, and a big thanks to Sam. Without you, we wouldn't have helped the frogs."

"The pond will be a good home for the tadpoles," said Mr. Johnson. "Come back soon and they will have turned into frogs."

"I will come back to see the frogs – as long as they don't turn into princesses!" said Sam, smiling.

Everyone laughed and laughed!